D1249374

Child's Guide to the Stations of the Cross

SUE STANTON

ILLUSTRATIONS BY ANNE CATHARINE BLAKE

FOUNTAINDALE PUBLIC LIBRARY

300 West Briarcliff Road
Bolingbrook, IL 60440-2894
(630) 759-2102

Paulist Press
New York/Mahwah, N.J.

To the Christians of the Holy Land
who walk their own Via Dolorosa
S.S.

For Nana, Bessie Brown
A.C.B.

Caseside design by Sharyn Banks
Caseside illustration by Anne Catharine Blake

Text Copyright © 2008 by Sue Stanton
Illustrations Copyright © 2008 by Anne Catharine Blake

All rights reserved. No part of this book may be reproduced or transmitted in any form or by any means, electronic or mechanical, including photocopying, recording, or by any information storage and retrieval system without permission in writing from the Publisher.

Library of Congress Cataloging-in-Publication Data

Stanton, Sue, 1952–
Child's guide to the Stations of the Cross / Sue Stanton ;
illustrations by Anne Catharine Blake.
p. cm.
ISBN 978-0-8091-6739-5 (alk. paper)
1. Stations of the Cross—Juvenile literature. I. Blake, Anne Catharine. II. Title.
BX2040.S83 2007
232.96'3—dc22

                                                                    2007020887

Published by Paulist Press
997 Macarthur Boulevard
Mahwah, New Jersey 07430

www.paulistpress.com

Printed and bound in Mexico

Hello. My name is John. Welcome to my church! I'd like to show you something very special to me. It begins with a story and a journey.

For over two thousand years, people have journeyed to the Holy Land to see where Jesus lived, died, and rose again. The journey is called a pilgrimage, and every place the pilgrims visit is called a station.

Many people could not make a pilgrimage. The Holy Land was too far away, or countries were at war. So the Stations of the Cross were created. This way, people who were not able to reach the Holy Land could still make the journey in their hearts.

The Stations tell us, in pictures, about the death of Jesus. At each Station we say a short prayer and study the picture. We think about the love Jesus has for us and how we may show that love to others. We pray an Our Father, a Hail Mary, and a Glory Be. We sing, and then we move on to the next Station.

For hundreds of years Christians have sung the *Stabat Mater* as they pray the Stations. This is Latin for "the mother stands." Many churches still sing this song during the Stations of the Cross, and we will too, joining with the Christians of old. With this song we stand alongside Mary. We share in her sorrow as she follows Jesus to the cross.

Now, let us begin our own pilgrimage with the Stations of the Cross.

FIRST STATION
Jesus Is Condemned to Death

We adore you, O Christ, and we praise you,
Because by your Holy Cross you have redeemed the world.

In the First Station, Jesus teaches us to be brave. Others have accused him of things that aren't true. The truth is that they are really accusing Jesus of loving people. Jesus loves everyone. He loves them completely, he loves them all the time, and he loves them just as they are. He tells us that this is the way *we* should love others.

At times it's tough to love others. It can be scary. People can be very unloving to us. People can hurt us. But Jesus says that this is what we must do. We should love others as God loves us. Every Station shows us exactly how Jesus lives his love.

I need to remember to love others, especially when someone hurts me or says things about me that are not true. I can defend myself, and I can tell others what happened. But I must also try to forgive people and try to love them. What I see in the picture of the First Station is that I must be like Jesus whenever I can.

Jesus, please make me brave enough to love as you do.

Pray an Our Father, a Hail Mary, and a Glory Be to the Father.

Sing, or pray silently:

> *At the cross her station keeping,*
> *Stood the mournful mother weeping,*
> *Close to Jesus to the last.*

Jesus Picks Up His Cross

We adore you, O Christ, and we praise you,
Because by your Holy Cross you have redeemed the world.

Jesus accepts the heavy cross he is given to carry. See how he stretches out his hands to accept it! There is no hesitation, no argument, no trying to hide from it. The cross is huge. No one looks able to carry it, and yet Jesus does. He carries a cross weighed down by our sin. He carries it because he loves us.

There are times when I do not want to accept *my* cross. Sometimes my cross is small, like when I have to do chores instead of watching TV. Sometimes my cross is big. I have to accept what I don't have and would like to have. This can be hard. It can be even harder to accept what I *do* have, like problems at school or at home. That's when I look at this Station. I don't see Jesus getting angry about his heavy cross. I don't see Jesus refusing to pick it up. I am thankful that mine is never as heavy to carry as his.

Jesus, please help me to accept my life.

Pray an Our Father, a Hail Mary, and a Glory Be to the Father.

Sing, or pray silently:

Through her heart, his sorrow sharing,
All his bitter anguish bearing,
Now at length the sword had passed.

THIRD STATION
Jesus Falls for the First Time

We adore you, O Christ, and we praise you,
Because by your Holy Cross you have redeemed the world.

Jesus suffers pain, and pain is a part of life. Illness is a part of life. Sometimes we recover from pain and illness. Sometimes we do not, or we do not recover entirely. Sometimes our thoughts are painful, too. We try not to worry, we try to forget, we try to change bad things into good. And we can't.

Even "little" pains hurt. We want to have fun all of the time. I know I do. I wish sometimes that I could stay at the amusement park forever, or at the pool, or in front of the TV or video game. But no matter how much fun I like to have, there is always an end to it and I must get back to real life, which can hurt. Then I look at this Station and see how Jesus endures great pain. He is patient. He is kind. He is forgiving. Even hurt, he is loving.

Jesus, please help me deal with my own pain, whether it is physical or mental or emotional. Help me to love others even when I hurt.

Pray an Our Father, a Hail Mary, and a Glory Be to the Father.

Sing, or pray silently:

> *O how sad, and sore distressed,*
> *Now was she, that Mother Blessed*
> *Of the sole Begotten One.*

FOURTH STATION
Jesus Meets His Blessed Mother

We adore you, O Christ, and we praise you,
Because by your Holy Cross you have redeemed the world.

Jesus sees his mother worrying about him. He can't help but see the pain in her eyes. He stops to talk to her. I am sure he tells her how much he loves her. He knows she wants only what is best for him, just like my family wants what's best for me.

But I forget this. I forget to tell my family how much they mean to me, how much I love them, and how much I want to thank them for being my family. When I look at this Station, I remember I should take the time to say "Thank you" and "I love you" to my family.

Jesus, I will remember how you comforted the ones who loved you.

Pray an Our Father, a Hail Mary, and a Glory Be to the Father.

Sing, or pray silently:

Christ above in torment hangs;
She beneath beholds the pangs
Of her dying glorious Son.

Simon of Cyrene Helps Jesus Carry His Cross

We adore you, O Christ, and we praise you,
Because by your Holy Cross you have redeemed the world.

Jesus accepts help from Simon to carry his cross. So many times, I think I can do things all by myself. I think I don't need advice or help from anyone. I think I have the answers to everything. But I really don't. I need to have help—from my parents, from my teachers, from my aunts, uncles, or friends. I need help to understand all the lessons in life I have to learn. We all do.

And Simon helps Jesus. At first he doesn't want to. He doesn't volunteer—he is just plucked from the crowd to help. That's how I feel sometimes. I'm being forced to be good. I'm being forced to do something that I am much too important to do. Let someone else do it!

But when I carry someone else's cross—even for a little while—I give that person more relief than I can ever imagine. When I look at this Station, I see Jesus being humble enough to accept help from others, and Simon being humble enough to help.

Jesus, please help me to always give help when I can and to accept it when I need it.

Pray an Our Father, a Hail Mary, and a Glory Be to the Father.

Sing, or pray silently:

> *Is there one who would not weep,*
> *Overwhelmed in sorrow deep,*
> *Christ's dear Mother to behold?*

Veronica Wipes the Face of Jesus

We adore you, O Christ, and we praise you,
Because by your Holy Cross you have redeemed the world.

Jesus receives compassion from a woman named Veronica. She sees a man who must be a criminal because he is going to be crucified. He is sweaty, dirty, and bloody. Yet she sees beyond that to the man's pain. The pain she sees on his face moves her—she sees pain, and yet a deep love as well. Surrounded by a screaming mob that could easily hurt her, she steps out of the crowd to help him. She stretches out her hands and wipes his face.

What courage! Veronica has no idea what might happen to her once she has wiped the man's face. She doesn't care. She feels only compassion for someone who is being bullied, beaten, and tortured. She may be frightened, but she helps him anyway. When I look at this Station, I see that being kind may be very hard to do. Sometimes it requires great courage.

Jesus, please help me have the courage to do the right thing even when I am afraid.

Pray an Our Father, a Hail Mary, and a Glory Be to the Father.

Sing, or pray silently:

> *Can the human heart refrain*
> *From partaking in her pain,*
> *In that Mother's grief untold?*

SEVENTH STATION
Jesus Falls for the Second Time

We adore you, O Christ, and we praise you,
Because by your Holy Cross you have redeemed the world.

Jesus perseveres and does not give in to his pain, but he falls a second time. He stands and picks up the burden of the cross again. This time there is no one else to carry it. It is *his* burden alone to carry, the burden of our sins. But his love for us is greater than that monstrous weight.

Many times I try to get rid of my burdens. I look for ways to get out of homework or out of chores I'm supposed to do around the house. As a result, I may fail my parents, fail school, fail the team, or fail myself. I could just lie down in my self-pity. Then I remember this Station and know I should pick myself up, put my hands back on my cross, and just like Jesus, keep on going.

Jesus, please help me to persevere even when it hurts.

Pray an Our Father, a Hail Mary, and a Glory Be to the Father.

Sing, or pray silently:

> *Bruised, derided, cursed, defiled,*
> *She beheld her tender Child;*
> *Skin with bloody scourges torn.*

EIGHTH STATION
Jesus Speaks to the Women of Jerusalem

We adore you, O Christ, and we praise you,
Because by your Holy Cross you have redeemed the world.

Jesus is kind to the people who have followed him, especially the women who cry as he passes them, carrying his cross. He stops to speak. Perhaps he first offers a prayer for them. And though he loves them in silence, he says something shocking: Do not cry for me, he says. Cry for yourself and your children.

It is not enough to be a bystander. It is not enough even to cry over other people's pain. Tears are easy. Action is not. Mere tears are like saying I want to be good, and then doing what's bad. They are like saying I'm sorry, and then doing hurtful things. They are like saying, yes, I will help, and then not helping. When I see this Station, I realize that good intentions are not enough. They must lead to good deeds. And good deeds can lead to changes in myself that may affect everyone I meet.

Jesus, please teach me to think good thoughts and then to do good deeds.

Pray an Our Father, a Hail Mary, and a Glory Be to the Father.

Sing, or pray silently:

> *For the sins of his own nation,*
> *Saw him hang in desolation,*
> *Till his spirit home was borne.*

NINTH STATION
Jesus Falls for the Third Time

We adore you, O Christ, and we praise you,
Because by your Holy Cross you have redeemed the world.

Jesus' pain is worse, and he falls again beneath the heavy cross. Yet he does not say a word about it. He has **accepted** his cross because of love for us.

Whether you realize it or not, there are always people who are living, right now, in some kind of pain—as close as your family, your school, and your church, and as far away as around the world. Sometimes you will be able to see what hurts these people. Sometimes their hurt is kept hidden inside. Perhaps, like Jesus, they have "fallen for the third time." Perhaps, at times, you feel that way yourself.

Don't be afraid to speak with people who live in pain. Take time to visit them. It is prayer in action, and a gift for both of you. For a few minutes both of you are lifted out of your suffering as you talk. At times you don't need to even speak, but just to sit quietly with the person. This Station reminds me that when people are in pain, it helps them to know that they are not alone—even when they've fallen for the third time.

Jesus, please help me to be kind to all those who may be suffering.

Pray an Our Father, a Hail Mary, and a Glory Be to the Father.

Sing, or pray silently:

O my Mother! Fount of love!
Touch my spirit from above;
Make my heart with yours accord.

TENTH STATION
Jesus Is Stripped of His Garments

We adore you, O Christ, and we praise you,
Because by your Holy Cross you have redeemed the world.

Jesus suffers shame and humiliation as his clothes are stripped from his body. He allows himself to be totally vulnerable as an act of love for us. And he stands alone in his vulnerability. There is no one in the crowd to stand with him.

People who suffer in war are vulnerable. Families who have been hit by disasters are vulnerable. The very young and the very old are vulnerable. People who endure chronic illness are vulnerable. When you face a bully, when you feel like your family is breaking apart, when you are confused and don't know what to do—you are vulnerable.

People who are totally vulnerable feel that they have been stripped of all that they had and all that they were. They don't realize that their true dignity and worth are on the inside and can never be stripped away. When I look at this Station, I know that Jesus is calling me to help the vulnerable and to clothe them with respect and dignity. When I recognize another's dignity, that person begins to understand that he or she is a child of God and deserves our respect.

Jesus, please help me to treat everyone I see with respect.

Pray an Our Father, a Hail Mary, and a Glory Be to the Father.

Sing, or pray silently;

Make me feel as you have felt;
Make my soul to glow and melt,
With the love of Christ my Lord.

ELEVENTH STATION
Jesus Is Nailed to the Cross

We adore you, O Christ, and we praise you,
Because by your Holy Cross you have redeemed the world.

Jesus stretches out his hands and is nailed to the cross. It is an acceptance of his earthly journey. It is also an embrace of every human being and every human sin.

Every life on earth has a time when it blooms and a time when it returns to God in heaven—even Jesus. Because of Jesus' love for us, because of his sacrifice on the cross, all life returns to God. When I look at this Station, I see Jesus showing us not to be afraid of, or to worry about, death. All life returns to God. What is more important, now, is how I use the life that God gives to me.

Jesus, please help me to value the great gift of my life and to use it as you wish.

Pray an Our Father, a Hail Mary, and a Glory Be to the Father.

Sing, or pray silently:

Holy Mother! Pierce me through;
In my heart each wound renew,
Of my Savior crucified.

TWELFTH STATION
Jesus Dies on the Cross

We adore you, O Christ, and we praise you,
Because by your Holy Cross you have redeemed the world.

Before Jesus dies, he says to God, "I put myself into your hands." What better way can there be to tell God, I trust you and I trust in your love for me? With these last words, Jesus leaves us with *faith*.

In this Station Jesus shows us that we are to always have faith in God's goodness and that not even death will stop the flow of God's love to us. What a wonderful gift to be thankful for—our faith.

Jesus, please help me to always have faith in God's love for me.

Pray an Our Father, a Hail Mary, and a Glory Be to the Father.

Sing, or pray silently:

Let me share with you his pain,
Who for all my sins was slain,
Who for me in torment died.

THIRTEENTH STATION
Jesus Is Taken Down From the Cross

We adore you, O Christ, and we praise you,
Because by your Holy Cross you have redeemed the world.

Jesus' friends take his body down from the cross. They show respect for the life it once held.

We experience our lives through our bodies. We can change the world only through the use of our physical bodies. We can relieve the suffering of others, offer food to the hungry, visit the sick, and pray for our enemies only by using our bodies. It is important to show respect for this creation of God's. When I look at this Station, I see how others respected the body of Jesus. I know that I am called to respect my own body and that of others.

Jesus, please help me to respect all life.

Pray an Our Father, a Hail Mary, and a Glory Be to the Father.

Sing, or pray silently:

Let me mingle tears with you,
Mourning him who mourned me too,
All the days that I may live.

FOURTEENTH STATION
Jesus Is Laid in the Tomb

We adore you, O Christ, and we praise you,
Because by your Holy Cross you have redeemed the world.

Just think of how hard it was for Jesus' family and friends to live without him. When someone you love dies, it is the most difficult time in your life. It is like wearing a coat of sadness that you can't take off. Suddenly the world stands still and seems like a very different place for you.

This must have been what it was like for the friends of Jesus. We are told they felt abandoned. We are told they felt afraid. What an awful time for them, and yet we know that God was still with them. When I look at this Station, I remember this. I remember that God is still with me too.

Jesus, please help me know that when I am afraid and feel alone, you are always there.

Pray an Our Father, a Hail Mary, and a Glory Be to the Father.

Sing, or pray silently:

By the cross with you to stay,
There with you to weep and pray;
This I ask of you to give.

FIFTEENTH STATION
Jesus Is Risen

We adore you, O Christ, and we praise you,
Because by your Holy Cross you have redeemed the world.

Many, but not all, churches have added a Fifteenth Station—the Resurrection! Jesus rises from the dead and brings us hope! Word spread quickly about the empty tomb. Imagine what disbelief, excitement, and finally joy the friends of Jesus felt! Jesus has conquered death. He promises us new life and fulfills his promise!

There are times when days seem very dark and scary, but now we have the word of Jesus. It is true. We have no need to be afraid of the dark any longer. Jesus is our new life and light.

Jesus, you are my hope and my light. Thanks be to God. Alleluia.

Pray an Our Father, a Hail Mary, and a Glory Be to the Father.

For this new Station, I've written a new verse for the *"Stabat Mater"* for you. Sing, or pray it silently:

Walk with me, O Mother Mild.
Bring me to your precious Child,
Jesus Christ, the Risen Lord.